A BRAGGING RIGHTS RECORD BOOK
for
Grandmas

BY BETH YARBROUGH

'BUT OF COURSE THEY'RE
WONDERFUL...
THEY'RE MY
GRANDCHILDREN!'

© Beth Yarbrough

© 2000 Havoc Publishing
San Diego, California 92121
U.S.A.

Artwork © 2000 Beth Yarbrough

ISBN 1-57977-165-3

www.havocpub.com

Made in Korea

A Positively UNBIASED RECORD of the MOST Perfectly Precious Grandchildren WHO EVER LIVED BY:

Contents

It's a Star-Studded Extravaganza!

Cute as a Button

Busy as a Bee!

Contents

As Sweet as Pie!

Snug as a Bug!

All I Want for Christmas!

IT'S A Star Studded Extravaganza!

The Grand Duchess
of
Kisses & Hugs

Photo of Grandma

My full name is: _____

My place of birth was: _____

I was (maybe) born on: _____

My grandchildren call me: _____

Before I became a grandmother, I was a pretty spectacular mom.

My children's names are: _____

_____

_____

Photo of Grandpa

The handsome prince, a.k.a.:

_____

who swept me off my feet...without whom

this book would never have been possible!

How Could They NOT be Fantastic?

Photo of Grandma
as a mom,
with children

Photo

Photo

Photo of parents
of grandchildren

Photo of parents
of grandchildren

Photo of parents
of grandchildren

Look who their parents are!!

A Star is Born!

Name: _____

Date of birth: _____

Time of birth: _____

Weight & height: _____

Parents: _____

Photo of grandchild

Grandma's totally objective journal account of one of the most splendid occurrences in modern history:

_____

_____

_____

_____

_____

_____

_____

_____

A Star is Born!

Name: _____

Date of birth: _____

Time of birth: _____

Weight & height: _____

Parents: _____

Photo of grandchild

The truth, the whole truth and nothing but the truth:

_____

_____

_____

_____

_____

_____

_____

A Star is Born!

Name: _____

Date of birth: _____

Time of birth: _____

Weight & height: _____

Parents: _____

Photo of grandchild

This just keeps getting better and better:

_____

_____

_____

_____

_____

_____

_____

_____

It's Marvelous!

Name: _____

Date of birth: _____

Time of birth: _____

Weight & height: _____

Parents: _____

Photo of grandchild

It's amazing!

_____

_____

_____

_____

_____

_____

_____

_____

Simply Unbelievable!

Photo of grandchild

Name: _____

Date of birth: _____

Time of birth: _____

Weight & height: _____

Parents: _____

But I saw it with my own eyes!

_____

_____

_____

_____

_____

_____

_____

Twinkle, twinkle, little star... _____

Grandma loves you just as you are! _____

Photos

Photo

Photo

Photo

Name: _____

Age: _____

Name: _____

Age: _____

Springtime, Sunday, Sunshine

All dressed up & impossible to resist!

Photo

Photo

Photo

Name: _____

Age: _____

Name: _____

Age: _____

Favorite springtime memories...

_____

_____

_____

_____

_____

_____

_____

_____

_____

_____

_____

_____

_____

_____

Magical Moments

Egg hunts, sprouting seeds, baby birds, buzzing bees

First encounters with the joys & wonders of life

Milestone
Memories

Photo

Graduations, Recitals...

...& milestones of note!

Photo

Photo

Photo

_____
_____
_____
_____

Graduations, Recitals...

_____
_____
_____
_____

Photo

...& milestones of note!

_____

Photo

_____
_____
_____
_____

Photo

Graduations, Recitals...

Photo

...& milestones of note!

Photo

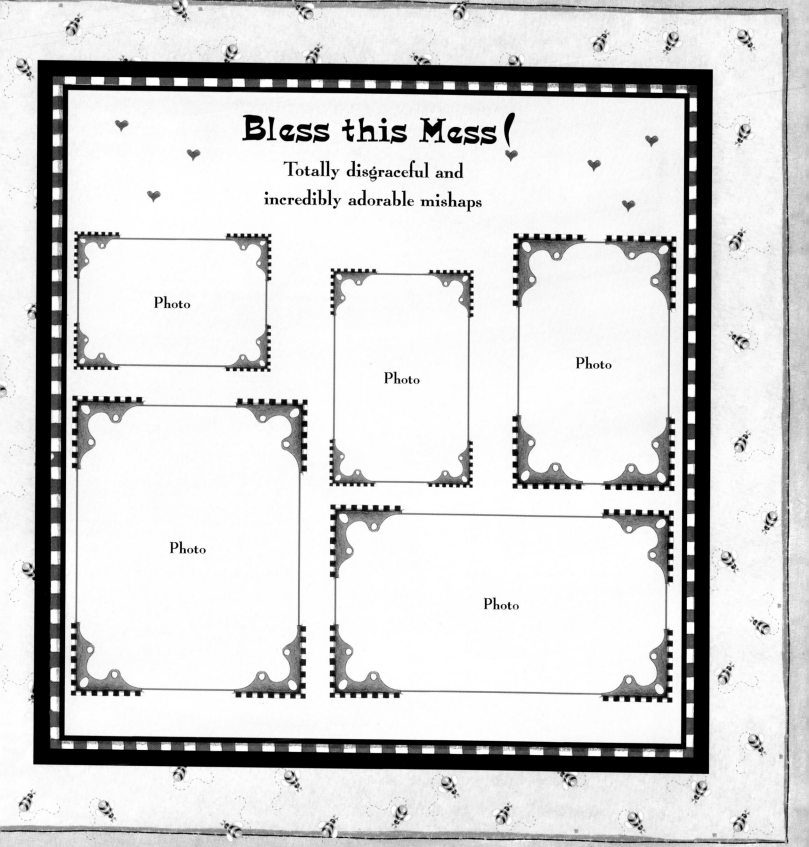

Bless this Mess!

Totally disgraceful and
incredibly adorable mishaps

Photo

Photo

Photo

Photo

Photo

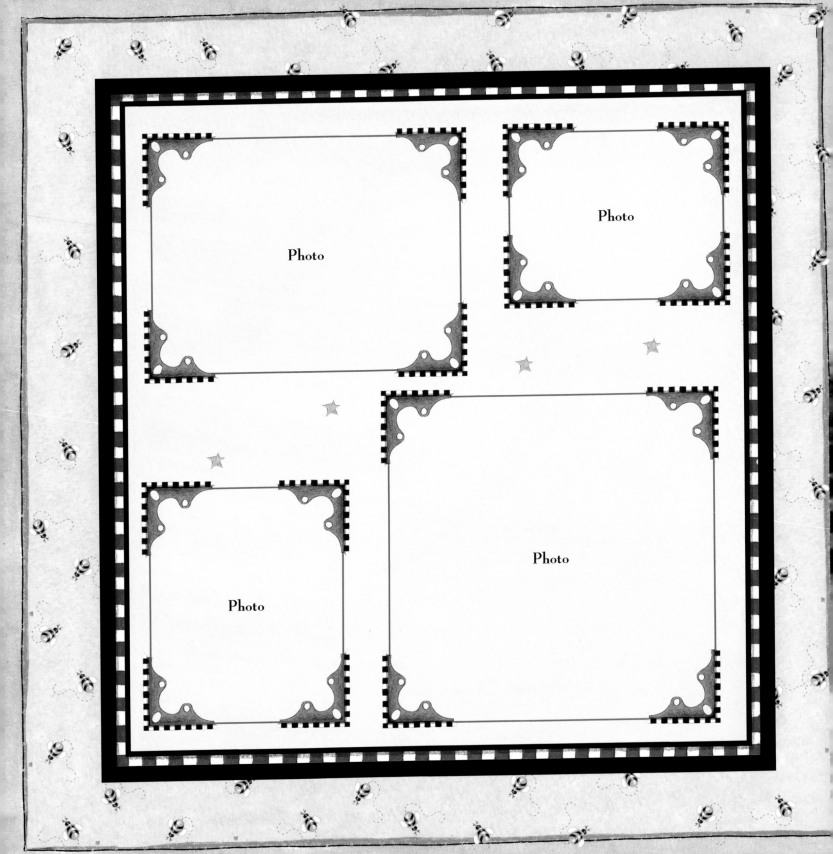

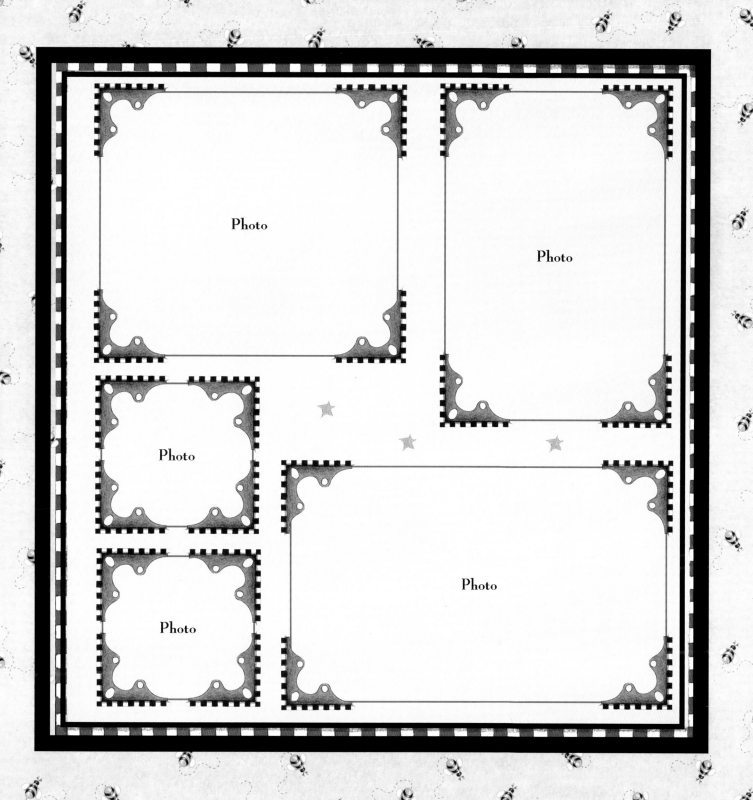

Someday They'll Hate Me for This

Tub Shot

Beach Shot

Diaper Shot

Towel Shot

Towel Shot

Free Shot

Bottoms Up!

GRAND ADVENTURES

Grandma's Diary

of vacations, parties, holidays, & assorted happenings

Photo

Photo

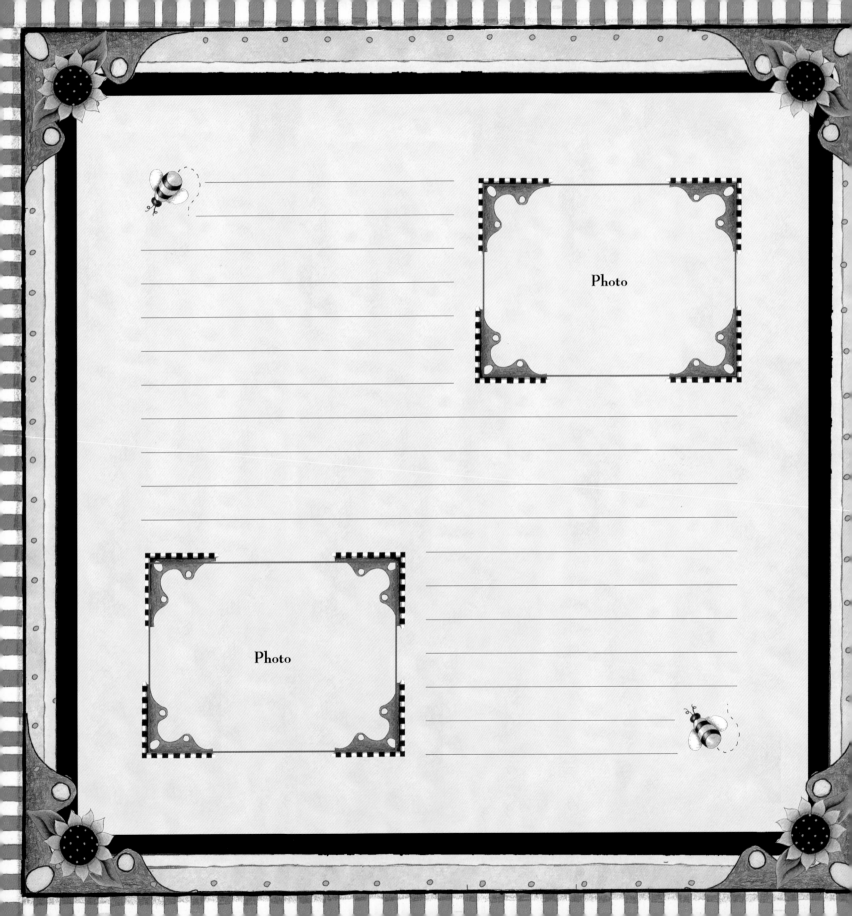

Photo

Photo

When I Grow Up

In their own words, what the most illustrious citizens of the world have planned for themselves...

Photo

Name: _____ **Age:** _____

_____

_____

_____

Name: _____ **Age:** _____

_____

_____

_____

Photo

Photo

Name: _____ **Age:** _____

_____

_____

_____

Photo

Name: _____ **Age:** _____

_____

_____

_____

_____

_____

Name: _____ **Age:** _____

_____

_____

_____

_____

Photo

_____

_____

Name: _____ **Age:** _____

_____

Photo

_____

_____

_____

When I Grow Up

In their own words, what the most illustrious citizens of the world
have planned for themselves...

Name: _____ Age: _____

Photo

_____

_____

_____

Name: _____ Age: _____

_____

Photo

_____

_____

Name: _____ Age: _____

Photo

_____

_____

_____

Photo

Name: _____ Age: _____

_____

_____

_____

_____

_____

_____

Name: _____ Age: _____

_____

Photo

_____

_____

_____

_____

Photo

Name: _____ Age: _____

_____

_____

_____

The APPLE NEVER falls very F·A·R from the

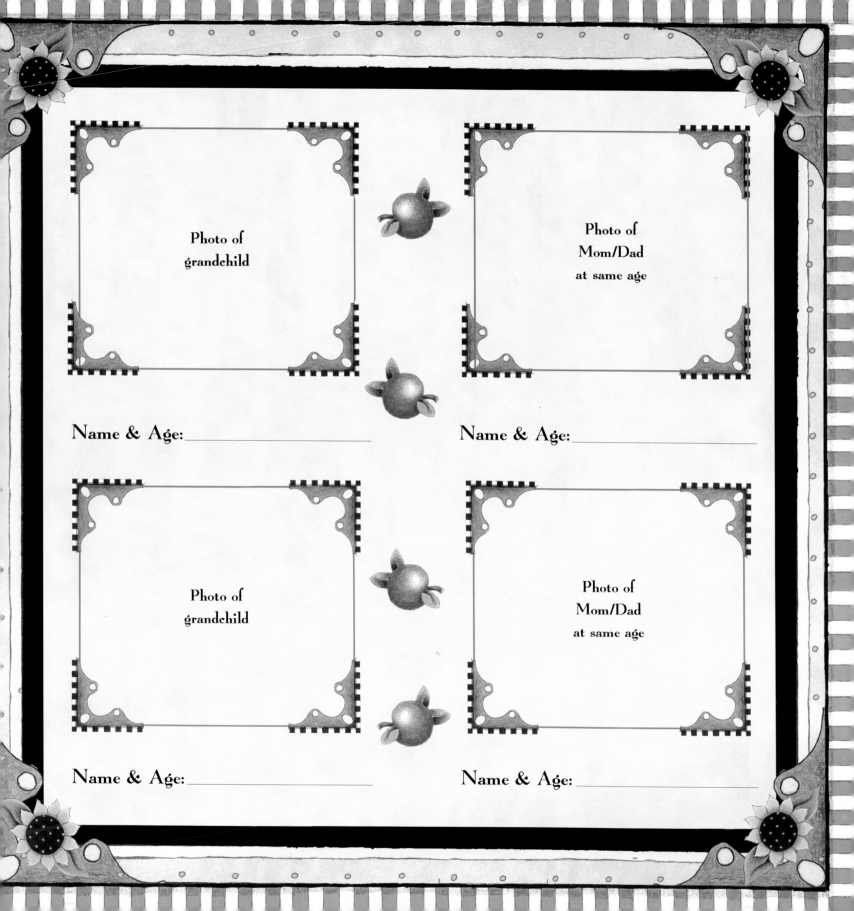

Photo of
grandchild

Photo of
Mom/Dad
at same age

Name & Age:_____

Name & Age:_____

Photo of
grandchild

Photo of
Mom/Dad
at same age

Name & Age:_____

Name & Age:_____

Photo of
grandchild

Photo of
mom/dad
at same age

Name & Age:_____

Name & Age:_____

Photo of
grandchild

Photo of
mom/dad
at same age

Name & Age:_____

Name & Age:_____

Say that Again

Memorable
Blabs,
Blurts
&
Mispronunciations

Say that Again

Guess Who·o·o?

©Beth Yarbrough

The Great Pumpkin Awards

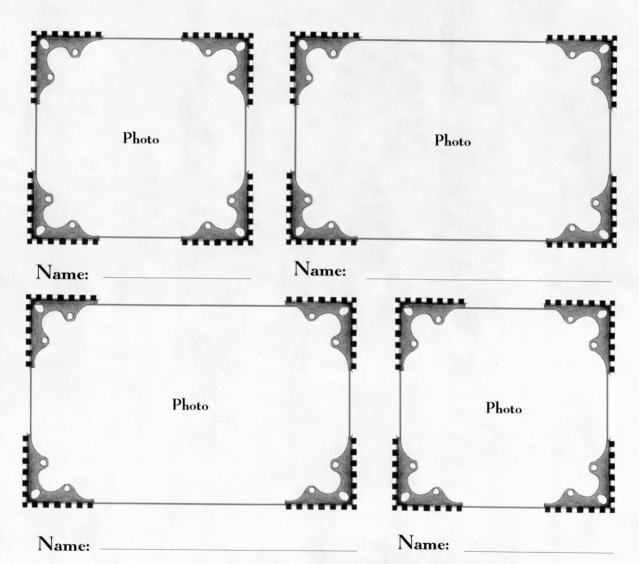

Photo

Photo

Name: _____

Name: _____

Photo

Photo

Name: _____

Name: _____

...and the Winner is...

Photo

Photo

If there is anything more irresistible
than grandchildren in the snow,
I'd like to know what it is!

Photo

Photo

Tender Treasures

The tattered tale of threadbare teddies, forlorn favorites & other fuzzies that made their days and nights just a little easier to bear

_____

_____

_____

_____

_____

_____

_____

_____

_____

_____

Photo

Photo

I'm not just saying that because they're mine.

Photo

Little Sweetheart!

Photo

Photo

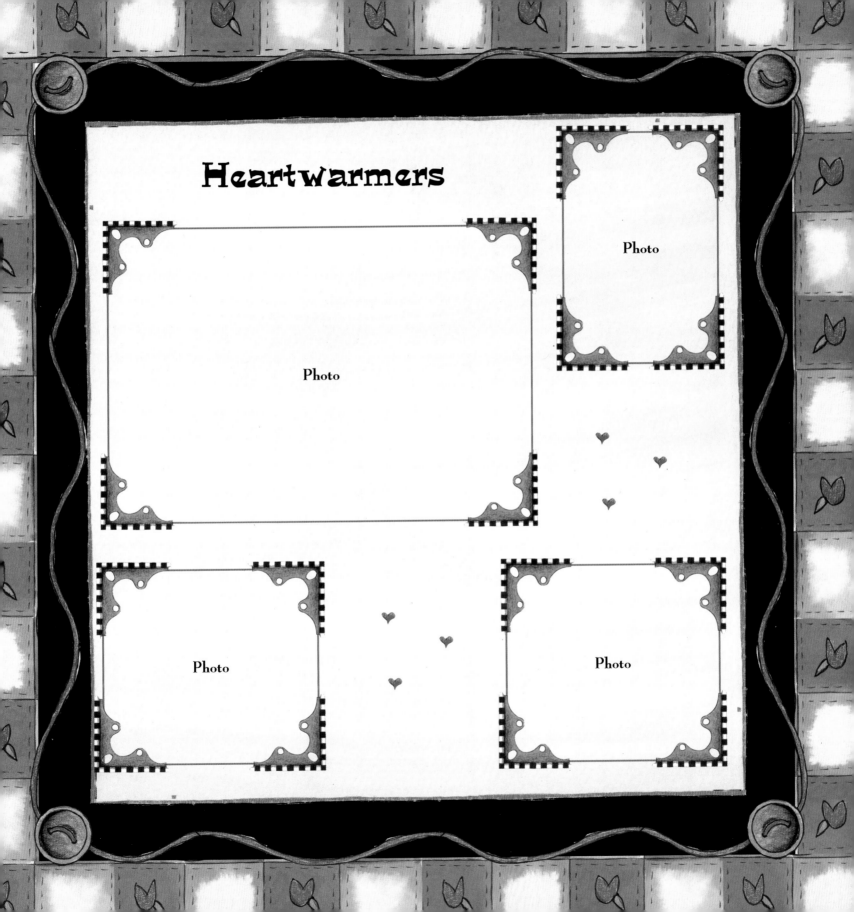

Heartwarmers

Photo

Photo

Photo

Photo

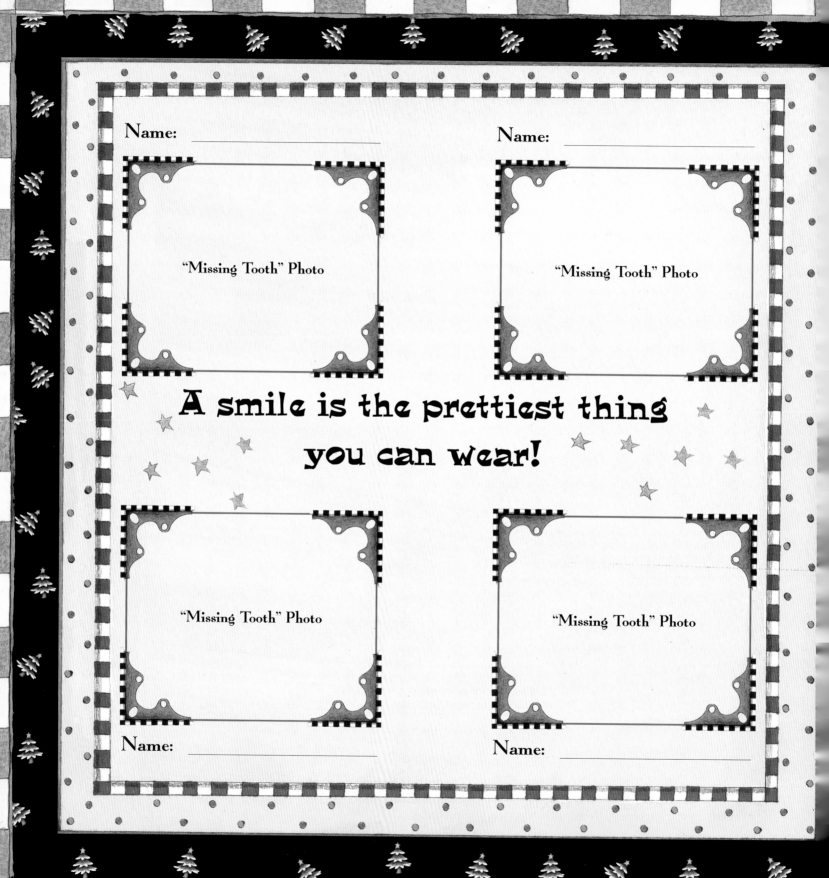

Name: _____

Name: _____

"Missing Tooth" Photo

"Missing Tooth" Photo

A smile is the prettiest thing you can wear!

"Missing Tooth" Photo

"Missing Tooth" Photo

Name: _____

Name: _____

all i want for Christmas...

©Beth Yarbrough

Dear Santa

Photo on
Santa's lap

Letter to Santa by: _____ Date: _____

Letter to Santa by: _____ Date: _____

Photo on
Santa's lap

The Holiday Herald

©Beth Yarbrough

Dear Santa

Photo on
Santa's lap

_____
_____
_____
_____
_____
_____
_____

Letter to Santa by: _____   Date: _____

_____
_____
_____
_____
_____

Photo on
Santa's lap

Letter to Santa by: _____   Date: _____

Christmas Morning

Grandma's Journal of the Entire Scene

Date: _____

_____

_____

_____

_____

_____

_____

_____

Photo

_____

_____

Photo

_____

_____

_____

_____

_____

_____

_____

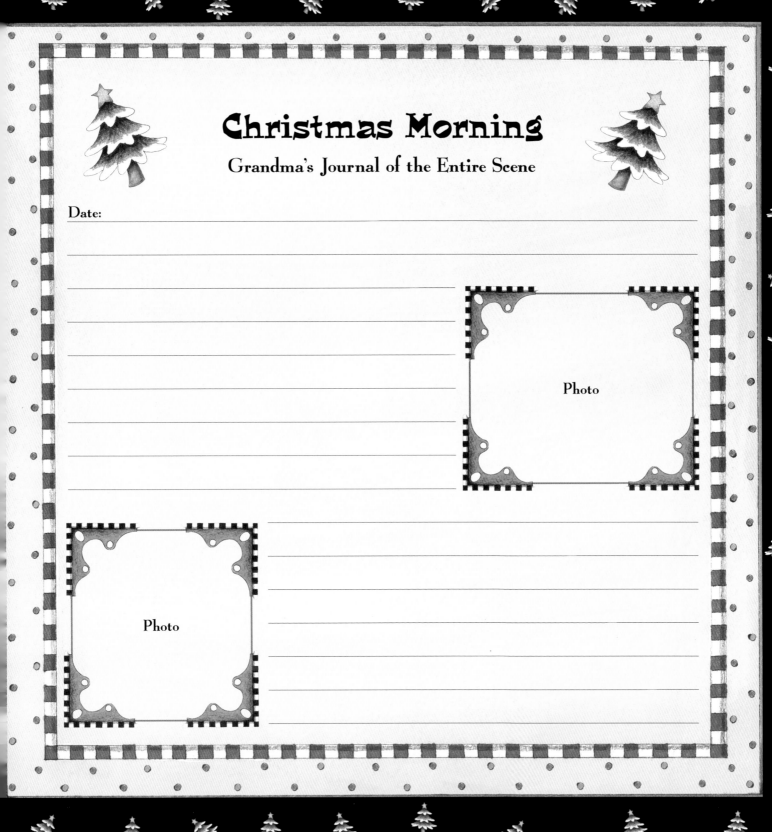

Christmas Morning

Grandma's Journal of the Entire Scene

Date: _____

_____

_____

_____

_____

_____

_____   Photo

_____

_____

Photo   _____

_____

_____

_____

_____

Christmas Morning

Grandma's Journal of the Entire Scene

Date: _____

_____

_____

_____

_____

_____

Photo

_____

_____

Photo

_____

_____

_____

_____

_____

The CHRISTMAS PAGEANT Chronicle

©Beth Yarbrough

Name: _____

Date: _____

Place: _____

_____

_____

Photo

Bloopers and Other Unscripted Disasters:

_____

_____

Photo

Name: _____

Date: _____

Place: _____

_____

_____

Bloopers and Other Unscripted Disasters:

_____

_____

_____

Name: _____

Date: _____

Place: _____

_____

_____

Photo

Bloopers and Other Unscripted Disasters:

_____

_____

_____

Photo

Name: _____

Date: _____

Place: _____

_____

_____

_____

Bloopers and Other Unscripted Disasters:

_____

_____

_____

_____